The INSIDE GUIDE

CELEBRATING NATIVE AMERICAN CULTURES

Native American Homes

By Trisha James

Cavendish Square

New York

Published in 2023 by Cavendish Square Publishing, LLC
29 E. 21st Street New York, NY 10010

Website: cavendishsq.com

This publication represents the opinions and views of the author based on their personal experience, knowledge, and research. The information in this book serves as a general guide only. The author and publisher have used their best efforts in preparing this book and disclaim liability rising directly or indirectly from the use and application of this book.

Disclaimer: Portions of this work were originally authored by P. V. Knight and published as *Native American Homes: From Longhouses to Wigwams* (Native American Cultures). All new material this edition authored by Trisha James.

All websites were available and accurate when this book was sent to press.

Cataloging-in-Publication Data
Names: James, Trisha.
Title: Native American homes / Trisha James.
Description: New York : Cavendish Square Publishing, 2023. | Series: The inside guide: celebrating Native American cultures | Includes glossary and index.
Identifiers: ISBN 9781502664280 (pbk.) | ISBN 9781502664303 (library bound) | ISBN 9781502664297 (6pack) | ISBN 9781502664310 (ebook)
Subjects: LCSH: Indians of North America–Dwellings–Juvenile literature.
Classification: LCC E98.D9 J36 2023 | DDC 392.3′608997–dc23

Editor: Therese Shea
Copyeditor: Jill Keppeler
Designer: Deanna Paternostro

The photographs in this book are used by permission and through the courtesy of: Cover Philip Lange/Shutterstock.com; pp. 4, 6, 8-9, 9 (inset), 19 courtesy of the Library of Congress; p. 10 Danita Delimont/Alamy Stock Photo; pp. 12-13 Hemis/Alamy Stock Photo; p. 14 File Upload Bot (Magnus Manske)/Wikimedia Commons; p. 16 JimCottingham/Shutterstock.com; p. 18 (main and inset) Zack Frank/Shutterstock.com; p. 20 Smit/Shutterstock.com; p. 21 Fæ/Wikimedia Commons; p. 22 Sopotnicki/Shutterstock.com; p. 24 Natalia Bratslavsky/Shutterstock.com; p. 25 Stillman Rogers/Alamy Stock Photo; p. 27 James Michael Dorsey/Shutterstock.com; p. 28 Yusiki/Shutterstock.com; p. 29 (left) Royal Geographical Society/Bridgeman Images; p. 29 (right) Stony River/Shutterstock.com.

Some of the images in this book illustrate individuals who are models. The depictions do not imply actual situations or events.

CPSIA compliance information: Batch #CSCSQ23: For further information contact Cavendish Square Publishing LLC, New York, New York, at 1-877-980-4450.

Printed in the United States of America

Find us on

CONTENTS

Chapter One: 5
　　More Than a Shelter

Chapter Two: 11
　　From the Earth

Chapter Three: 17
　　Homes of Wood

Chapter Four: 23
　　Native American Homes Today

More to Explore   28

Think About It!   29

Glossary   30

Find Out More   31

Index   32

Swiss artist Karl Bodmer traveled the American West in the 1830s creating pictures of Native American life, such as this image of the inside of a Mandan leader's home.

MORE THAN A SHELTER

What does "home" mean to you? When you really think about it, it probably means many things. Sure, it's the place where you sleep, which you share with your family. It's also the place where you eat meals and celebrate special occasions such as birthdays and holidays. It can give you shelter in bad weather and also provide comfort after a hard day.

Home was all these things to Native Americans who lived long ago, too, just as it is today. Also, just as people's homes can look quite different today, not all early Native American homes looked alike. Different groups of Native Americans built different kinds of homes, depending partly on the natural resources around them.

Fast Fact

Weather was a consideration with Native American homes. It can be more than 100 degrees Fahrenheit (38 degrees Celsius) in the Arizona desert and colder than −40°F (−40°C) in the Arctic!

From Nature

When people build homes today, they might have certain requests about what the home should be made of, such as brick or wood. However, they probably don't even think of whether these materials are available around

This 16th-century engraving shows homes in a Secotan village located in North Carolina.

them. Construction materials can be shipped anywhere in the world now.

Of course, years ago, that was not the case for Native Americans. They had to use the natural resources that existed around them to make most things, including their clothes and homes. Some groups used bison hides or other animal skins. Some used tree trunks, branches, bark, and grass. Others used earth and mud. Still others used adobe blocks and stone. In the cold Arctic areas of the North, some used snow and ice.

Tepees

A group's way of life also shaped Native American homes. Some groups lived in settled villages, so they spent time making permanent homes.

THE ALL-IMPORTANT BISON

Bison (sometimes called buffalo) were extremely important to Native Americans of the Great Plains, including the Lakota, Blackfoot, Crow, and Arapaho. They needed the large animals for food, clothing, tools, and building materials. Bison hides were used as a covering for homes. When white settlers moved west in the 1800s, the bison population fell sharply due to overhunting, disease, and other factors. In a few decades, tens of millions of bison were reduced to about 300, according to some estimates. They almost became extinct. While the species was saved, the peoples who depended on bison suffered and lost a key part of their traditional life.

Fast Fact

Bison were so important that they were a feature of some Native peoples' religions.

Other groups were **nomadic** and needed homes they could make quickly or carry with them. The tepee, or tipi, may be the most recognizable of traditional Native American homes.

The home of most nomadic Plains peoples, the tepee had a cone-shaped frame made of wood. It could shelter a whole family. The frame was constructed of about a dozen long poles that were stuck in the ground to form a circle about 12 to 16 feet (3.7 to 4.9 meters) wide. About 15 bison hides were used to cover the frame. Since fires were burned inside the tepee, an opening was left at the top to let smoke out.

Tepees were usually made by the women of the community. They prepared the poles, made the hide covering, put up the tepees, and took them down when preparing to move again. They also decorated the inside with pictures.

An entire village could have tepees packed and ready to move within an hour.

Fast Fact

The door of a tepee was often a bison hide with the hair still on it or a bearskin.

Some Native Americans used tepees during hunting season and came home to earth lodges, like those shown here.

FROM THE EARTH

Chapter Two

Not all Plains peoples lived in tepees year round. Some were farmers who raised crops and needed homes that would last. They built strong, sturdy earth lodges. The Mandan people who lived along the Missouri River in today's North Dakota were one such people. An earth lodge was home to 15 to 25 people, and a Mandan village often had 12 to more than 100 lodges.

The frame of an earth lodge was made of 10 to 15 large posts arranged in a circle 20 to 50 feet (6 to 15 m) across. Four taller posts were set in the center. A hole was left in the roof of the lodge to let smoke out and light and air in. Beams were laid across the tops of the posts. Long poles with woven branches covered the beams. Then, hay and earth covered the whole thing. The entrance was through a short hall.

Fast Fact

Today, the Mandan, Hidatsa, and Arikara Nation—called the Three **Affiliated** Tribes—live on the Fort Berthold Indian **Reservation** in North Dakota.

Hogans

The Navajo of Arizona and New Mexico moved to the Southwest from the North and brought a style of housing with them that differed from the homes of other Native Americans of the Southwest. They lived in hogans.

To build a hogan, the Navajo first dug a shallow pit in the ground. (Building partially underground offered protection from harsh weather.) Then, they set up a frame using posts made from the tall piñon, a pine tree. Finally, the frame was covered with plants and earth. A short hall led to the entrance, which usually faced east and the rising sun and was covered with a blanket. Like other early Native American homes, hogans had an opening in the top to release smoke from fires burned inside.

Hogans had no walls inside and no windows.

Wattle-and-Daub Houses

Native Americans originally of the Southeast, such as the Cherokee and Creek (Muscogee), were farmers and hunters who wanted homes that would last. They built what are often called wattle-and-daub houses.

The term "wattle" has to do with the frame of the house. It was made of poles, or wattles, stuck into the ground, and then woven with branches

Fast Fact

The Cherokee called wattle-and-daub houses *asi*.

This picture shows a rebuilt wattle-and-daub house.

PIT HOUSES

A pit house is just what it sounds like: a house built in a pit, with half of it below the surface of the ground. This type of home was found in parts of Washington, Oregon, Idaho, Montana, and California. The Nimiipuu (Nez Perce) and Klamath are two peoples who lived in them.

The pit house had a log frame. The walls and roof were covered with grass, sticks, bark, and other plant matter and then covered with earth. The smoke hole in the roof was also the entrance, and people climbed down a ladder to get to the floor. In some places, pit houses were connected by tunnels, which were used during cold, snowy winters.

and vines. The word "daub" refers to the matter that was used to coat the frame. It was made with mud, clay, sand, chalk dust, dried grass, and even animal waste. The roof of a wattle-and-daub house was covered with grass, bark, or cane mats. It was constructed to shed, rather than absorb, the heavy rains of the Southeast climate.

A wattle-and-daub house usually lasted 10 to 15 years, and a village might consist of as many as 80 such homes. Some peoples, including the Cherokee, surrounded their wattle-and-daub villages with a palisade, or a fence of wood stakes, to protect them from enemies.

Several families lived in a plank house.

HOMES OF WOOD

Native Americans who lived in or near forested areas used more wood in their homes. The Northwest Coast has towering red cedar trees, and the Native Americans there used these to build their homes. These dwellings got their name—plank houses—because they were made of planks, or wooden boards, tied to wooden frames.

The houses were large, sometimes up to 60 feet (18 m) wide and longer than 150 feet (46 m). They had no windows, but planks in the roof could be moved to let light in. Smaller houses were often just one large open room, but they were sometimes divided by mats hung from beams. Larger houses usually had several rooms but not always.

Fast Fact

Plank houses were usually built over an **excavation** 1 foot (30 centimeters) or more deep.

The Chinook people who lived in today's Oregon and Washington State often had more than one plank house frame and moved seasonally, from summer to winter villages. They removed the planks from one house frame and traveled with them to the other village.

Longhouses

Haudenosaunee (sometimes called Iroquois) of the Northeast lived in settled villages and farmed, hunted, and gathered their food. They built longhouses for several related families, called a clan, to share. A longhouse had a frame of poles made of saplings and an arched roof where the poles were tied together. The dwelling could be from 40 feet (12 m) to more than 200 feet (122 m) long and more than 20 feet (6.1 m) wide. Sheets of bark covered the frame and were tied in place.

In longhouses, men and women often had separate doors, one at each end of the house.

The large area inside was divided into rooms, like apartments. Walls were lined with bunks. Top bunks were for storage, while lower bunks were for sleeping. One or more holes in the roof allowed fire smoke to escape.

Wickiups

Other peoples of the North built smaller homes in a similar manner as longhouses were constructed. These are often called wickiups (or sometimes wigwams). "Wickiup" (from the Fox language) and "wigwam" (from the Abenaki language) both mean "dwelling."

Peoples of the Northeast, Plains, Great Basin, Plateau, and California regions built wickiups, as they were easy to construct.

IGLOOS

What about Native Americans who didn't have bison hides, trees, long grasses, or similar resources to make homes? Some Arctic peoples lived in homes that were like pit houses, with frames of whale bone. Famously, some Inuit made dwellings called igloos out of snow.

Traditionally, Inuit men built the igloo, also called *iglu* or *aputiak*. It took at least two people to build one. They had to choose the snow carefully so that it wasn't too hard or too soft. Women and children filled in holes and spaces between the blocks of snow. A tunnel-like entrance led into the igloo.

Igloos aren't as common now but are still constructed on hunting expeditions.

Like longhouses, wickiups had a bent sapling frame tied at the top. Mats of bark, animal hides, blankets, or woven **rushes** covered the frame. A wickiup was usually about 20 feet (6.1 m) across. Wickiups weren't as difficult to build and were used by nomadic peoples.

Chickees

The Seminoles of Florida needed homes suited to the hot wetlands of the **Everglades**, where they built villages in the early 1800s. They constructed a special type of home called a chickee.

The chickee's frame was made of thick posts, often logs from the cypress tree. Palm leaves covered the roof. The wooden floor was 3 to 4 feet (0.9 to 1.2 m) above the ground and was accessed by ladder. The raised floor kept mud, water, and snakes out of the home. Hide or cloth walls were sometimes added to keep out the rain, but most of the time, the sides remained open to the warm weather.

Fast Fact

Seminoles in northern Florida made more permanent log cabins.

The chickee's pointed roof was made from palm leaves tied together with grass, rope, or vines.

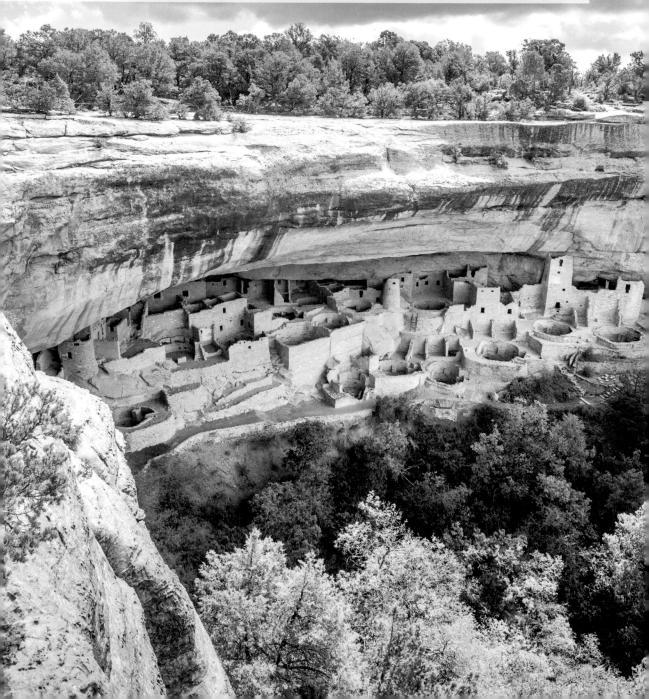

Pueblo dwellings started with the cliff dwellings of the Ancestral Pueblo, the ancestors of today's Pueblo peoples. The Cliff Palace at Mesa Verde National Park in Colorado, shown here, is an example of this type of housing.

NATIVE AMERICAN HOMES TODAY

Today, most Native Americans live in towns and cities and in the same kinds of homes other Americans live in. However, some live on their **ancestral** lands, sometimes in the traditional-style dwellings of their ancestors. A few even live in the *same* buildings that their ancestors called home long, long ago.

Pueblos

Native Americans in the deserts of the Southwest lacked the abundance of wood that Native peoples in the East had. They constructed connected homes called pueblos. The early ones were built of stone, but later homes were built of adobe blocks. The stone pueblos were made with sandstone blocks held together with a mix of mud and water. The adobe pueblos had a frame of wooden posts and beams. Adobe bricks were laid around the frame and held together with a mix of mud and water.

Fast Fact

Pueblo buildings were up to five stories tall.

Each pueblo house had an entrance in the roof, which was reached by ladder. Ground-floor rooms were usually for storage. Each floor above it was set back a little, so the entire structure looked a bit like a pyramid with steps. Each family usually lived in a single room in the pueblo, although side rooms could be added.

Acoma, shown here, is sometimes called Sky City. It's located on a mesa, or flat-topped hill, 357 feet (109 m) high.

SENECA BARK LONGHOUSE

The Seneca Bark Longhouse at Ganondagan State Historic Site in Victor, New York, was constructed in 1997 on the site of a Seneca community that was destroyed in the late 1600s by French leader Marquis de Denonville. The house was built to look just like a 1670 longhouse and includes objects created by Seneca craftspeople. The Seneca Bark Longhouse offers visitors opportunities to learn about the Seneca and the other Haudenosaunee peoples in an **authentic** setting. The Seneca Art and Culture Center, also on the 569-acre (230 hectare) site and completed in 2015, presents more exhibits that explore Haudenosaunee society.

Visitors can tour the inside of the Seneca Bark Longhouse and imagine what life was once like for the Haudenosaunee.

Preserving the Past

Sadly, much early Native American **architecture** hasn't survived to the present day. War, weather, and the natural breakdown of construction materials have largely erased early Native American homes from the landscape. In addition, many Native peoples were pushed off their lands and pressed to abandon their customs, including building traditional homes.

Archaeologists and historians are still interested in looking for the remains of early Native American homes, however. For example, in Colorado, more than 330 wickiup sites dating back to the mid to late 1800s have been identified. Researchers hope that, by identifying sites, the wickiups can be placed on the National Register of Historic Places, helping to preserve them. Additionally, some Native American homes that remain—such as those at Mesa Verde—are protected as state or national historic sites.

Many Native communities today are still building traditional houses for special events or purposes such as meeting halls. Some construct these houses to teach about their history. A few peoples, like the Navajo and Pueblo, continue to build their traditional homes simply as homes, wishing to live like their ancestors. In this way, they honor, respect, and pass down the customs of their cultures to the next generation and ensure that this part of their traditions isn't lost to time.

Some Navajo **elders** still live in hogans, though the ones built today use different construction materials. They're usually built in the shape of a hexagon or octagon.

Where These Homes Were Found

igloo
plank house
pit lodge
earth lodge
tepee
pueblo
hogan

wickiup
longhouse
wattle-and-daub
chickee

This map shows where these Native American homes were most common.
But the tepee and wickiup, for example, were found in other places too.

1. If you had to use local natural resources to build a new home, what could you use?

2. Which kind of traditional Native American home would best suit your family? Why?

3. Name some challenges to building some kinds of traditional Native American homes today.

4. Why do you think some Native groups still build traditional structures for their community meeting houses rather than a different kind of building?

GLOSSARY

affiliated: Closely connected to something as a member.

ancestral: Having to do with ancestors, or people who lived before others in a family.

architecture: A style of building or construction.

authentic: Made the same way as the original.

elder: One who has authority due to experience and age.

Everglades: A swamp region in Florida.

excavation: The act or process of digging and removing earth.

Great Basin: A region in the western United States that includes much of Nevada and Utah and parts of Idaho, Oregon, California, and Wyoming.

nomadic: Having to do with people who move from place to place.

reservation: Land set aside by the U.S. government for Native Americans to live on.

rush: A tall grasslike plant that grows in wet areas, sometimes used to make things when it's dried.

FIND OUT MORE

Books

Grover, Kevin, and Wilma Mankiller. *Do All Indians Live in Tipis? Questions and Answers from the National Museum of the American Indian*. Washington, D.C.: Smithsonian Books, 2019.

McNeese, Tim. *Native American America: North America before 1492*. New York, NY: Rosen Publishing Group, 2021.

Websites

Chickee
www.semtribe.com/stof/culture/chickee
Discover the history of the chickee according to the Seminole people.

Chinookan Plank Houses
www.oregonencyclopedia.org/articles/chinookan_plank_houses/#.YiuhmO7MKAw
Learn much more about these interesting dwellings.

Native American Houses
www.native-languages.org/houses.htm
See photos and read descriptions of the homes in this book.

INDEX

A
Abenaki, 19
adobe, 6, 23
Arapaho, 7
Arctic, 5, 6, 20
Arikara, 11
Arizona, 5, 11

B
bison, 6, 7, 9, 20
Blackfoot, 7

C
California, 15, 19
Cherokee, 14, 15
chickees, 21, 28
Chinook, 17
Colorado, 22, 26
Creek, 14
Crow, 7

F
Florida, 21
Fox, 19

H
Haudenosaunee
    (Iroquois), 18, 25
Hidatsa, 11

hogans, 11, 12, 13,
    27, 28

I
Idaho, 15
igloos, 20, 28
Inuit, 20

K
Klamath, 15

L
Lakota, 7
lodges, 10, 11, 28
log cabins, 21
longhouses, 18, 19,
    21, 25, 28

M
Mandan, 4, 11
Montana, 15

N
Navajo, 11, 12, 26, 27
New Mexico, 11, 24
Nimiipuu (Nez Perce),
    15
North Carolina, 6
North Dakota, 11

O
Oregon, 15, 17

P
pit houses, 15, 20, 28
Plains peoples, 7, 11,
    19
plank house, 16, 17,
    28
Pueblo peoples, 22,
    26
pueblos, 23, 24, 28

S
Secotan, 6
Seminole, 21
Seneca, 25

T
tepees, 6, 7, 8, 9, 10,
    11, 28

W
Washington, 15, 17
wattle-and-daub
    houses, 14, 15, 28
wickiups (wigwams),
    19, 21, 26, 28